G000166810

PRESENTLY

First published in 2022 by Kingston University Press.

A catalogue of this book is available from the British Library

ISBN 978 1 909362 64 2

Typeset in Garamond

Photographs/artwork © Simon Tyrrell

Additional photography by Marisa Spence (Pages 24, 26, 27, 28) and Astra Papachristodoulou (Page 57)

Editorial and design by Kingston University MA Publishing students: Aishwarya Rajak, Aríel Bertelsen, Karin Markovič, Marisa Spence

KINGSTON UNIVERSITY PRESS
Kingston University
Penrhyn Road
Kingston-upon-Thames
KT1 2EE

@associatetyz | www.tyrrellknot.com | @tyrrellknot

PRESENTLY

Simon Tyrrell

KINGSTON UNIVERSITY
PRESS

For my dear wife Helen Nicholas
and dear friend Steven Fowler.

Without you,
I'd be neither
the person
nor poet
I presently am.

CONTENTS

WHAT AM I DOING HERE?

For context, I am presently here, writing this. Presently, you shall be there, reading it. When you are there, you shall refer to where you are as here.

What are you doing here?

> I pray you all that be present
> That you will here with good intent
> And let your ears be lent
> Heartful, I you pray

I've no idea what I'm doing here.

> It's a mystery. Something difficult or impossible to understand. A craft. My series of actions habitually performed.

Where to start?

Alpha. In the beginning. The word.

I've always worked with words. After lengthy spells pressing them into the service of others' interests, I've more recently come to use them to serve my own creative endeavours.

> *Pay attention. It's all about paying attention.*
> *Attention is vitality. It connects you with others.*
> *It makes you eager. Stay eager.*
> Susan Sontag

I've long been interested in how the relationships people have with their community are captured and codified in customary practices. It's in this that I've found the opportunity for my poetic practice, which typically celebrates the distinctive language, stories, marks and symbols people have used to present, protect and promote their community and make sense of the relationships, time and space they share. Those communities might be technical, cultural, geographic: real or imagined.

But I'd also long been concerned that my instinctive passion for language-referent art and visual literature would likely leave me outside of any group that might share my interest and encourage my endeavour.

I first met Steven J Fowler in mid-January 2017, when he was bringing his work with Kingston University's literary cultural institute – Writers' Centre – out into its surrounding community. I was exploring ways to expand my own engagement with the broader creative and academic population as part of a local community interest company's endeavours to build community well-being and resilience. I'd recently helped to establish The Museum of Futures as the first physical manifestation of their work to provide safe stimulating spaces for the community's ideas to thrive: liberating the natural brilliance and creativity of those eager to contribute to shaping the future for themselves and those around them.

Within a month we'd together launched the first in what became the most regularly well-attended programme of exhibitions and events hosted by The Museum, not only partnering Writers' Centre for four busily productive years, but also a rich range of other associated ventures. The European and Nordic Poetry Festivals, Poem Brut, English PEN, Camarade and Enemies Project all continued to draw in not only university students, staff and alumni, but a broad community of practising writers, emerging and well-established, often with considerable national and international reputations.

These truly enabling encounters found me increasingly participating in the midst of a generous, inclusive, unconventional, and celebratory community of remarkable, creative and productive folk, whose progressive good-willed practice manifestly contributed to my creative evolution. Visual poetry and performance were soon providing the opportunities I'd long sought to expand my own endeavours to bring together and celebrate seemingly separated things I'd previously thought I alone cared for.

It's been a joyful privilege to find a rare depth of friendship and fellowship across this rich and supportive ecosystem of practitioners, organisers, publishers and engaged and inquisitive spectators who share an interest in historical and contemporary visual literature and innovative performance practice. It's expanded my community, the permissions I knew I never really needed to be as productive as I'd always hoped and offered access to the support and resources I need to explore sharing the work I make more widely.

I'm wearing a hat, we're poets and a rose is a rose.

What's become clear is that the sustainable well-being of those communities dwelling in the material that I am mining for my work, as well as those we call our own, requires the relationships at their heart to be performed – participated in, rather than spectated. My work explores the potential to participate vicariously in recognising, celebrating and venerating communities other than our own – an opportunity to sense 'belonging', albeit temporarily, to another community of interest.

In its making and performance I try always to guard against the kind of affectation, habit and tic that might hinder us inhabiting others' worlds, and pursue more authentically distinctive ideas, marks and gestures that might instead help.

Which is where this book comes in, so fittingly produced as part of a genuinely collaborative participatory endeavour with Kingston University's Writers' Centre and postgraduate students working towards a masters in publishing, for Kingston University Press.

'Presently' is a collection of 14 performances, rooted in a poetry I've come to understand through Steven J Fowler's own compelling take: 'language art where the miracle of language itself can be turned away from expediency... [a poem is] a fragment of the marks and sounds we communicate with... which does not necessarily aim to be informative or communicative... a burst of the miraculous (Seen as Read, 2021)'.

In regarding all that I devise as 'objects that include text', I happily acknowledge Ian Hamilton Finlay's work as a particular touchstone, celebrating the wit that was his wisdom's constant companion:

'THING' POEMS – There is a difference between a poem which is 'about' a thing and a poem which is a thing – its own thing, but not necessarily without reference to something else.

All performances here were devised for a specific event. Several have been associated with exhibitions of visual poetry to which I've contributed work, drawing on the theme of the exhibition and, on occasion, related to and explicitly referencing my visual poetry contribution. Others have been for specific 'poetry in performance' events, some of which were part of the Writers' Centre Kingston annual programme, some the European Poetry Festival, others were Poem Brut events. Visual material accompanying the text here includes visual poems from those exhibitions, items produced as part of a performance, or props. I've done minimal editing, for example adding 'stage directions' to relate text to prop on the few occasions those are central to the storytelling, and without which the text would simply be ungrounded or abstract.

This is their first appearance on the page but they are neither properly 'scripts' nor 'transcripts' and I'd like to think that it's more than simply a collection of one form in another. They are perhaps instead documenting poetry which has here been staged for the page. As all aspects of my work share preoccupations and inquiry, my aim is to place performance alongside my visual poetry as part of a coherent poetic practice. While performances are inevitably transient, the work in them is not necessarily ephemeral. I'm keen not only that the work itself has a life beyond the transitory performance for which it was derived, but that this book explores the potential for a documented performance to be a piece of work in and of itself, standing alone or elaborating on other products of my practice. Staged for the page.

> Presently we'll be *ad fini.*, near the end, which
> will no doubt feel like *ad inf.*, at infinity.

So, a collection of documentary objects that I hope are authentically distinctive, rooted in a poetry staged for the page falling somewhere between habit, tic and affectation and bursts of the miraculous.

Omega

> 'Reading next will be Simon Tyrrell'
>
> [Wearing a black bowler hat]

BOUGH, BOW, BOW

[Wearing a black bowler hat]

A contextual reading from *With a Bended Bow*, on bended knee:

'On the head of a ship in the front, which mariners call the prow, there was a brazen child bearing an arrow with a bended bow. His face was turned toward England and thither he looked as though he was about to shoot...

Cognizances, liveries, badges and standards: Cognizances were means of visual identification... while nobles were identified by their arms on shields, banners and surcoats, the lower classes were identified by group.'

[Using a curved branch to represent]

I am a tree, this is my bough.
I am an archer and this is my bow.
I am a boat and this is my bow.
I am a poet and this is my hat.

[Removing the hat]

I am a poet of Briton currently working in English.

[Drawing cards from the hat, each visibly bearing the word defined]

This is my 'bough' – the main branch of a tree.

This is my 'bow' – a weapon for shooting arrows, made of a curved bit of wood, joined at both ends by a taught piece of string.

This is my 'bow' – the front end of a boat.

This is my 'bow' – cause to bend with age or under a heavy weight.

And this is a 'bow' – a bend of the head or upper body as a sign of respect, greeting or shame.

This is Poem Brut.

This is a tree.

This is an archer.

This is a boat.

This is to bow.

This is to bow.

If this is a tree, then this is a bough.

If this is an archer, then this is a bow.

If this is a boat, then this is a bow.

This is Poem Brut, this is the poem.

[Visibly scribing symbols to represent]

Tree bough
Trees bow
Trees' boughs
Trees bow
Bows bow
Archer's bow
Archers' bows
Bows bow
Archer's bow bows
Boughs bow
Boughs bow
Archers bow

From that bough comes this bow and this bow.

If that is a tree, and that is an archer and that is a boat, then this is a poet.

And this is the poet's last bow.

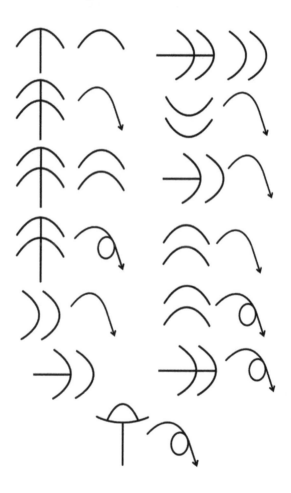

THE ROSE OF THE NAME

Contextual readings for today's name-calling, from Gertrude Stein's poem *Sacred Emily*, written in 1913:

'Rose is a rose is a rose is a rose'.

When asked what she meant, she said that in the time of Homer, or of Chaucer, 'the poet could use the name of the thing and the thing was really there'.

From a selected list of varieties, published by The National Rose Society in 1964 – the year of my own naming:

A handbook intended as a guide for amateurs, to assist them in making a selection most suitable for any particular purpose.

Contains descriptions of the best, and also varieties which are most suitable for various purposes.

Lists are offered as a guide to the less experienced, some may be suitable for towns, industrial areas or other unfavourable positions.

In the lists they are divided, most are also suitable, the following may be mentioned.

It may be found that some old favourites have been excluded.

Some names *of* Roses:

Alberic Barbier
Betty Uprichard
Conrad Ferdinand Meyer
Elsa Arnot
William Lobb
Ena Harkness
Ritter von Barmstede
Kathleen Harrop
Lucy Cramphorn
Meg Merrilees
Frau Dagma Hastrup
Stella
Uncle Walter
Violinista Costa
Paddy McGredy
Faust

The above have a natural tendency in Great Britain as given.

What's in a name? That which we call a rose
by any other name would smell as sweet.

Fragrance is often in the individual appreciation by the observer.

This is Poem Brut

Here are roses for some names.

    [indicating roses in vase]

Here are some names *for* roses.

    [distributing labelled roses]

Tallyho!

Picture

The People

My Choice

Brilliant

Vanity

Optimist

Happy

Lively

Joyfulness

    Suspense

    Message

Dearest

Celestial

Angel Wings

Bashful

Buccaneer – *for Steven J Fowler*

Mischief

    Grumpy

Superstar

Firecracker

Blaze

Oh La La

Dominator

Siren

Scandal

Pax

Simple Simon – *for me*

Ballet

Ballerina

Rumba

Circus

Independence

Fashion

Elegance

Enterprise

Prosperity

Miracle

Sleepy

Parade

Serenade

Purity

Highlight

Memoriam

Peace

Thanks to Peter Abelard

'The name of the rose is meaningful to the
understanding, although there are now no roses
remaining.'

EGO SUM ALPHA ET OMEGA

[Enter carrying a printer's type tray, swinging a
censer charged with acetone. Reverently place
tray on a table and coloured ink pads in the
compartments for a, e, g, h, l, m, o, p, s, t and u.
Genuflect]

A contextual summoning to the mysteries:
  Lordings royal and reverent
  Lovely ladies that here be lent
  Sovereign citizens hither am I sent
  A message for to say
  I pray you all that be present
  That you will here with good intent
  And let your ears be lent
  Heartful, I you pray

  Ego sum alpha et omega
  Primus et nobilissimus
  It is my will it should be so
  It is, it was, it shall be thus

And some revelations of a printer's devil we meet
in a mystery play:

  I am a poor devil, and my name is
  Titivillus. I must each day bring my
  master a thousand bags full of failings
  and of negligences in syllables and words.

Born at the fall of Lucifer – before time begins.

Ego sum alpha et omega
The first and the last
The beginning and the end

It's a mystery:

> Something difficult or impossible to
> understand or explain

> The secret rites to which only initiates are
> admitted

> The Eucharist

> A handicraft or trade

But our 'fount' contains all the answers.
From the French for casting, and Latin for melt –
it's a printer's font where alpha and omega prevail
as glyphs.

Each glyph must be even in appearance with
every other glyph regardless of order or
sequence. Each glyph consists not only of
the shape of the character, but also the white
space around it.

In the manufacture of metal type, a 'matrix' is
the mould used to cast a letter – from the Latin
meaning womb or a female breeding animal

Alpha

In the beginning was the word

And the word became flesh.

> This is my body, that is, the figure of my
> body. A figure, however, there could not have
> been, unless there were first a veritable body.
> An empty thing, or phantom, is incapable of a
> figure
>
> the thing that is signified is effected by its sign
>
> in, with, and under the forms.
>
> Do this in remembrance of me.

Omega

The printer's devil takes worn and broken lead type
to the hellbox for melting and recasting.

This is Poem Brut

My series of actions habitually performed
Upside down, back to front
Minding my p's and q's

> [Finger-printing from the ink pads in the
> compartments of the type tray that correspond
> to the letters]

e g o
s u m
a l p h a
e t
o m e g a

The thing that is signified is effected by its sign
– in, with, and under the forms.

Printing is a mystery – from the beginning to the end.

Here is my proof.

MEMENTO MORI

I've no idea what I'm doing here.

I thought I might remember someone to you. One of these two men here:

This one:

Neither of them I remember.

Two great-grand-something-or-other-to-me
Tyrrells served in the First World War.
Horace a private in the 17th Lancers and Harry a
driver in the Royal Field Artillery.

Horace died. Harry survived.

I've brought mementos: coins, medals, a note.
I'm doing 'numismatics' – studying coins, medals,
tokens and things that settle things.

Some of which are technically referred to as 'odd
or curious.'

The Kyrgyz people used horses as their principal
currency unit and gave small change in lambskins
– lambskins may be suitable for numismatic study,
horses are not.

A coin's value to collectors generally depends on
its condition, historical significance, rarity, quality
and popularity. A coin greatly lacking in these is
unlikely to be worth much.

I have made a catalogue.
To 'coin' we invent or design a new word or phrase.
Coin comes from Old French for 'wedge, corner,
mint and die'.
To die is to stop living, to be forgotten.

A George III shilling from 1816.
To 'take the King's shilling' was
slang for joining the armed forces –
'earnest' money to seal the bargain
of recruitment – exchanged for a bounty that was
used to equip yourself.
A private's pay was a shilling a day – expected to
cover food and clothing.
In 1847, a limit was placed on deductions – so
each soldier received at least a penny.

Pip, Squeak and Wilfred was a cartoon published
in the *Daily Mirror* from 1919.
Pip was a dog, discovered begging on the Thames
Embankment, sent to a dogs' home and bought
for half-a-crown – two shillings and sixpence.
Squeak, was a penguin from London Zoo
and Wilfred a rabbit with long ears adopted by Pip
and Squeak.

The Charge of the Light Brigade was a failed
military action against Russian forces in the
Crimean War in 1854. It involved the 17th Lancers.
The 17th Lancers would have taken the Queen's
shilling.

A shilling from 1853
and the penny they were
guaranteed.

MEMENTO MORI

The 17th Lancers' motto – 'death or glory' – is
featured on a death's head badge on cap and collar.
670 men rode out. 118 were killed, 127 wounded,
60 taken prisoner.
335 horses died.
More death than glory.

> Half a league, half a league,
> Half a league onward,
> All in the valley of Death
> Rode the six hundred.
> 'Forward, the Light Brigade!
> Charge for the guns!' he said.
> Into the valley of Death
> Rode the six hundred.

It wasn't 'six hundred', but 'six hundred and
seventy' doesn't scan.
From 1879, the bounty for the Queen's shilling
ceased, recruits were encouraged to keep a shilling
for luck instead… and Kipling petitioned for a
shilling kindly dropped in a little tambourine.

Tennyson's 'The Charge of the Light Brigade'
was the first and only poem I learned to recite, at
primary school.

The Dickin Medal is the highest award any animal
can receive whilst serving in military conflict – for
acts of bravery or devotion to duty – a large,

bronze medallion with 'For Gallantry' and 'We
Also Serve' in a laurel wreath.
It's been awarded to 34 dogs, 32 pigeons, four
horses and one cat.

 Horace and Harry would have taken the
King's shilling

and these pennies a day for
service in the First World War.

Custom dictates that remembrance
need be poetic:

It is sweet and fitting to die for one's
country
Greater love hath no man than this
He had done good towards God and
toward his house
Gave the most that men can give – life itself

'The Old Contemptibles' was coined for those
British servicemen who served from 1914 or 1915.
They were awarded three medals.

 Horace's 1914 Star
and the note accompanying his British
War Medal and Victory Medal that
'would have been conferred had he
lived in memory of services'.

It's already being called the 'Great War' in the note, and 'The Great War for Civilisation 1914–1919' on the Victory Medal.

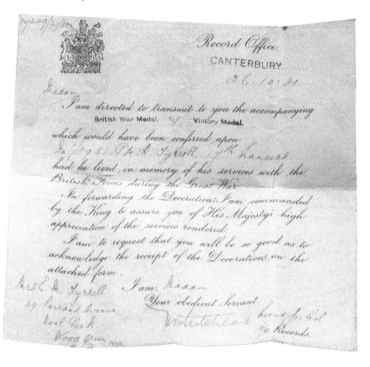

Yes, 1919 – and they were distributed in 1921. Obedient servant Whitehead Lieutenant for Colonel in charge of records 'requested that you will be so good as to acknowledge the receipt of the Decorations on the attached form'.

A memorial bronze plaque was sent to next-of-kin of service personnel who were killed. Horace died for 'Freedom and Honour'. Death not glory.

The name does not include the rank – sacrifice knows no distinction.

The plaque became known as the Dead Man's Penny and the medals as Pip, Squeak and Wilfred.

For God for King and country

For loved ones, home and empire
for the sacred cause of justice and the
freedom of the world
we shall remember them
their name liveth for evermore

I thought I would do something to commemorate Horace with my 'mementos' – souvenirs to 'bring him to remembrance'.

Something that is odd and curious...

The badge on cap and collar says these are all 16th Lancers.

No death or glory to see here.

This man

is not actually in this photo.

There's writing on the back. But it's football fixtures.

And none of them may be Horace or Harry.

I have no idea who these men are.

I've no idea what I've done here.

I'll never forget.

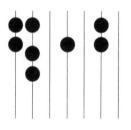
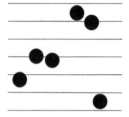

Jetons are impelled   Ha'pennies are shoved

RECKONING BETWEEN THE LINES

Romans played games by placing counters on or between lines carved on a board. The board was called a 'table'.

Medieval and renaissance accountants did their reckoning by placing 'jetons' on the lines carved on a board, like an abacus. The board was called an 'abacus'.

Shove ha'penny players shoved ha'pennies between the lines carved on a board. The ha'pennies are called 'ha'pennies', the board is called a 'board'.

Roman gaming tables had exhortations to good civic and gaming behaviours.

Medieval and renaissance jetons had exhortations to good commercial and moral behaviour.

Neither the board nor the ha'pennies in shove ha'penny carried exhortations.

The only thing written on a shove ha'penny board were the scores in chalk.

I wanted to add exhortations to shove ha'penny and thought I might do something with chalk – but it makes my teeth go funny.

Instead, I rewrote some of the rules of shove ha'penny, replacing the word 'board' with exhortations from roman tables, and 'ha'penny' with exhortations from jetons.

Off – The start of a game.

Away – A call to warn a player that his scoring Happiness (luck or fortune) comes from God alone, is occupying a circus is crowded; ear-deafening cheers; the gates are shattered already filled and will be awarded to his opposition.

Lay – A Truth succeeds over all so positioned on the Holy fatherland; grant that I may see my loved ones safe that by playing a Fortune given is not guaranteed directly behind it, that Luck or fortune and glass how soon they break, will score. To take a lay or hold a lay.

Cannon – Causing an Envy does oneself harm, to strike another and score but in so doing causing the struck The Word of God remains eternal, to travel forward and score against a further Diligent accounting makes for correctness.

Draw – To play a Love me as I love you in such a way that it scores without touching another To float. To paint. To dewdrop. Rare.

Thick – When a God's blessing brings riches, is covering too much of The Parthians slain; the Briton defeated; play Romans! to provide a lay.

Thin – Opposite of **thick**.

Bed – The scoring area between the vertical and horizontal lines of the You're a bad player, when you lose you cry, when you win you rejoice.

The dee – An obsolete area adjoining the top virtue of The Empire; the enemies are in chains; Roman's play! where, in an older version of the game, a player had to score a Red today, dead tomorrow, before he could start the game proper.

Tight – A God's Kingdom remains eternal, that is too close to a line to score. Requiring a **tickle** or **touch**.

Tickle – To strike a God's Word remains eternal, gently with another causing it to travel sufficiently forward where it had been previously touching a line.

Touch – Same as a **tickle**.

Parish – The area of the circus is crowded; the cheers of the people; the joy of the citizens, where scores are still required.

Brushed – Beaten by one or more empty the enemies defeated; Italy rejoices; play, Romans! Empty Stand up! Go Away! You're a bad player, back out idiot!

Scudds – A rather unkind expression, but you may hear worse, un-sportingly said under one's breath, meaning that you hope your opposition fails to score.

Virgin Mary – To score with all five Whoever trusts in God has (not built on a sand foundation) by floating or drawing. That is no five Happiness comes from God, is true. Come into contact with each other, Isle of Wight.

Chalks – Lines in chalk recorded on the edge of the to hunt, to bathe, to play, to laugh; this is to love, to indicate how many One should praise God's gifts have been scored.

Bring back shot – Causing any To God alone the glory to strike another in such a way as to cause it to travel backwards.

Shot – The playing of at the beginning consider the end. A turn or hand. An expression meaning 'Good shot'.

BLUEPRINT FOR THE TRANSCRIPT OF A DRAFT

BLUEPRINT FOR THE TRANSCRIPT OF A DRAFT

I have donned a smock to protect my clothes
during the messy stages of drafting.
An interpretative edit of the blueprint for an
unfinished draft of a poem what I wrote – Bon
voyage. It's called 'Bon voyage'. The performance
contains mild peril.

[Indicating step stool]

Bon voyage

[Facing stage rear for ~~deletions~~, standing on
step stool for ^insertions, moving across stage
for {^insertions} of text from elsewhere on the
blueprint]

We saw three ships come sailing ~~by on the~~ ^sea
fields of blue
~~foam-flecked~~ ^clipping {^at pace} the foam-
flecked swell
~~foam-flecking~~
~~the illegible swell~~
~~{^Shanty man's }~~ there were gusts
but all was well

two boats we saw a-driving by
~~ploughing~~ {^unrigged through}
fields with bells of blue
keels hauled the arterial tributaries
keels hauled the arterial tributaries
fields with bells of blue
{^~~with~~ tacking}
tightbound ^graceless to wagons on wheel
against {^land's} pitch, roll and yaw
{^heedless of winds prevailing}

landbound tributaries
~~arterial~~ ^along routes prescribed ~~illegible~~ {^hedge
and hard shoulder}
Needless of tack or jibe
~~Illegibly-hyphen-illegibling~~

til crow and kestrel ~~hand~~ over the watch
to cormorant and gull
~~as~~ and the coast wets its welcome

BLUEPRINT FOR THE TRANSCRIPT OF A DRAFT

SOME MATERIAL CONSIDERATIONS

I am the keeper of knowledge accidentally advocating a fitting future over five minutes for a friendship.

Words are very important to us. We'd ask that everyone listen very carefully because that's how we've chosen them… if recent history indicates anything we might expect others to play with words, sometimes placing them in other's mouths.

Say what you see, to save what can be seen – some material considerations in words from other's mouths.

Mute Swan, Canada Goose, Egyptian Goose, Shelduck, Gadwall, Teal, Mallard, Shoveler, Red-crested Pochard, Pochard, Tufted Duck, Pheasant, Cormorant, Grey Heron, Little Grebe, Great Crested Grebe, Black-necked Grebe, Sparrowhawk, Kestrel, Moorhen.

> The water by Hampton Court was believed to possess medicinal properties, as efficacious in the gravel for kidney stones, excellent for drinking and washing.

At Kingston on Thames and Surbiton – New Kingston, a populous and increasing place – the want of water is much felt. About half a mile from the bowling-green at the west end of the town is a spring that is cold in summer, and warm in winter – it bubbles up, and is called Seething Well. The Inhabitants thereabout do use to wash their eyes with it, and drink of it.

Monster Soup commonly called Thames Water being a correct representation of that precious stuff doled out to us, brought forth all monstrous, all prodigious things, hydras and organs and chimeras dire.

The water taken from the River Thames at Chelsea for the use of the inhabitants of the western part of the metropolis, being charged with the contents of the great common sewers, the drainings from dunghills and laystalls, the refuse of hospitals, slaughterhouses, colour, lead and soap works, drug mills and manufactories, and with all sorts of decomposed animal and vegetable substances, rendering the said water offensive and destructive to health, ought not to be taken up by any of the water companies from so foul a source.

A portion of the inhabitants of the metropolis are made to consume, in some form or another, a portion of their own excrement and, moreover, to pay for the privilege.

It is become little short of compulsory upon all classes to provide themselves with abundant supplies of pure wholesome water.

Coot, Lapwing, Dunlin, Snipe, Common Sandpiper, Green Sandpiper, Black-headed Gull, Mediterranean Gull, Common Gull, Lesser Black-backed Gull, Herring Gull, Great Black-backed Gull, Common Tern, Stock Dove, Woodpigeon, Collared Dove.

I feel confident no other site or source can be found, which combines so many advantages, and from which so pure, constant and abundant a supply can be obtained with so small an expenditure.

The water at Ditton being usually very clear, would be passed at once from the river by conduit pipes to filters, from them to the wells of the pumping engines, and then through aqueduct or main pipe to reservoirs. The filtering apparatus will be erected on such a principle, that the water must of necessity pass at all times through the filtering medium before it can reach the pump-well of the steam-engines.

A peculiar power possessed by porous media of removing matter from solution in water.

Undulating layers of fine sand, coarse sand, shells (from Harwich), fine gravel, coarse gravel. The *schmutzdecke* or filter skin contains microorganisms and bacteria that break down and digest organic matter in the water and consume dead algae and living bacteria.

There should be a presumption in favour of physical preservation of nationally important remains.

Industrial archaeology is being lost during the development of post-industrial society. Because many of these sites lie on valuable and desirable riverside sites they are in danger of being totally eliminated from the built environment. The site is therefore particularly sensitive.

Ring-necked Parakeet, Swift, Kingfisher, Green Woodpecker, Great Spotted Woodpecker, Magpie, Jay, Jackdaw, Carrion Crow, Gold Crest, Blue Tit, Great Tit, Sand Martin, Swallow, House Martin, Long-tailed Tit, Chiffchaff.

SOME MATERIAL CONSIDERATIONS

The banks of the river at Seething Wells on a fine day are worth a visit, for the busy and animated scene there presented. It is impossible for anyone unacquainted with the plans of the undertaking to form any judgement of what will be the eventual condition which the spot is to assume, but at the pace now maintained order and effect will soon emerge from the present temporary chaos and confusion – above 800 men are now engaged and over £1,000 was disbursed last week for wages alone.

It is a matter for great satisfaction that in the congregation of such a number of individuals engaged at the work, such a small cause for complaint has been given on the score of irregularity or disturbance. Indeed their conduct has hitherto generally been exemplary.

The cholera was fourteen times more fatal amongst the persons having the impure water of the Southwark and Vauxhall Company, as amongst those having the purer water from Thames Ditton.

Seventy-five species of bird and eleven species of bat visit, roost, breed, hibernate or forage.

Blackcap, Whitethroat, Reed Warbler, Wren, Starling, Blackbird, Song Thrush, Redwing, Mistle Thrush, Robin, Wheatear, Dunnock, House Sparrow, Tree Sparrow, Grey Wagtail, Pied Wagtail, Meadow Pipit, Chaffinch, Greenfinch, Goldfinch, Reed Bunting, Black Swan.

A glorified duck pond.

64 floating homes, a 90-berth marina, a 110-diner restaurant and 184 parking spaces.

Both parties had a 'relaxed' approach to honest dealings when it suited them... [He] clearly is an extremely aggressive businessman who made his fortune operating petrol stations in the East End and is prepared to use any bullying tactic possible to secure what he wants... His performance as witness was masterly, however in my view it bore no relation to the way in which he performs outside the court... a carefully constructed charade and in no way reflects his true persona.

Local support or opposition for a proposal is not in itself a ground for refusing or granting planning permission and such support does not justify the harm that I have identified above.

It is both patronising and contrary to the whole
spirit of the importance now attached to local
views for the Appellant to try and argue that
the claimed benefits for the local community
override the clear harm, in circumstances where
the local community have reached a clear view
to the contrary by a significant majority.

Praise some although they knew not what they did.

Do not forgive others for they know exactly what
they do.

Wild Scabious, Trefoils and Clovers, Small
Scabious, Reflexed Stonecrop, Dropwort,
Restharrow, Fern Grass, Broomrape, Spanish
Broom, Ladies Bedstraw, Bir Buttercup, Black
Medick, Mouse Eared Hawkweed, Pipistrelle,
Noctule, Daubenton's, Brand, Leisler, Serotine,
brown Long-eared, Natterer.

Sun's on the lagoons.

ORIGINS

My work celebrates the distinctive language, signs and symbols that people use to establish, present, protect and promote their community and make sense of the relationships, time and space they share – those communities might be technical, cultural, geographic: real or imagined.

No surprise I was delighted to be invited to participate in this beautiful project, reflecting on how a community might distinctively establish and present itself when surrounded by water.

If we're talking about the customary language that helps us form relationships with the time and space we share on land, we've archaeology to thank for gifting some delightful language to help – my favourites are:

> *terminus post quem* – the earliest time something may have happened or found itself at a particular location, and

> *terminus ante quem* – the latest.

But if archaeology offers much to the historians of communities on land, we need other lexicons when space is less tangible and immutable and time is harder to tell... as it is for those communities on the water.

Fortunately, I have a sign drawing on the
magnificent, authoritative *Sea-Lore* from
1929, which offers some traditional – not
at all inappropriate or culturally insensitive
– observations about how we might efficiently
explain to each other:

> how to leave enough space between ourselves
> and something else to be sure of our safety

> where we stand when we make decisions about
> staying still or moving off

How to:

> mark time in the absence of light

> assign responsibility for safeguarding our
> compatriots

> report progress on our journey

> hand over duties to those taking watch
> while we turn in for a night in our assigned
> accommodation

How do we know we're going in the right
direction, and when we've arrived where we
intended?

Sea-Lore asks, 'where are we to begin or leave off?'
and suggests, 'it is confessedly difficult...'

'The wise would have the courage to prefer the
right word to another
which may be both clumsy and incorrect'
'For a landsman to use the shellback's
pronunciation would smack of affectation...'

So, let us:

Stand off, a whole nine yards
'til a **good offing, before the mast**
weighs *in a* **couple of shakes, off and on**
to **flog the glass**
'til the **bell** *calls* **dog-watch** *end*
and the **dead reckoning** *of a* **clean slate**
lets us **pipe down** *to* **closed quarters**
as a **jury rig** *means we won't* **lose way** *or*
wash out *but,*
instead **let go** *to* **lee**
'til arrival is heralded by the welcome sight of a
Leading light

LAYING CLAIM

For context, I am presently on land.

Presently, I shall be on water.

A contextual citing of Susan Sontag:

> Be clenched, curious. Not waiting for
> inspiration's shove or society's kiss on your
> forehead. Pay attention. It's all about paying
> attention. Attention is vitality. It connects you
> with others. It makes you eager. Stay eager.

Rose is a rose is a rose is a rose... the poet could
use the name of the thing and the thing was really
there.

> The thing that is signified is effected by its
> sign – there cannot be several things exactly the
> same, for in that case there would not be several
> things, but the same thing itself. Therefore,
> all things both agree with and differ from one
> another.

Seeing the same things, and seeing things the same
– depends on your point of view.

A short performance reflecting on a visual poem
what I wrote – called 'Laying claim' – with props.

land	bank	open land
water	river	open water
land	bank	open land

riverbank	river's bank	on land
river	river water	on the river
riverbank	river's bank	on land

land	water	vehicle
lake	waterlocked	watercraft
land	water	vehicle

community
river community
community

[Indicating a blue scarf which will represent
'water' and a miniature telescope-topped walking
cane which will represent 'point of view']

Some things are on water, others on land.

We see things on water, from on land.

And things on land, from on water.

Some are on water, as if from on land.

Say, what do you see?

'Blind' is to be unable to see, acknowledge, perceive.

> It is without regard to evidence or prior knowledge
>
> It is failing to produce flowers
>
> It can be a destination sign or something to conceal some covert deed or design; to mislead the eye or the understanding, a subterfuge
>
> It can be without seeing, unseeingly
>
> Absolutely, totally, I'll swear... it can be any device intended to conceal or hide.

Do you say what you see or see what you say?

land, **water**, land

open land, **open water**

if **a river**, then a bank

if **a river**, then sometimes the riverbank

then again sometimes it's the river's bank, but always and only ever **river water**

when on land... it's a vehicle

but on **water**, a **watercraft**

[Pooling the scarf]

when this is land, this is a **lake**

[Winding the scarf around neck]

but when this is land, this land is **waterlocked**

[Tapping head]

here it's always community – from here that's only ever a **river community**

Do you say what you see or see what you say?

The poet could use the name of the thing and the thing was really there... the thing that is signified is effected by its sign.

Be clenched, curious... Attention is vitality. It connects you with others. It makes you eager. Stay eager.

HERE AND THERE

For context, I am presently here.

Presently, I shall be there.

When I am there I shall refer to where I am as 'here'.

We tend only to need names for places when we're not there – 'where are you from?' asks the Saxon of the Celt near what was to become Ashby de la Zouche.

'*Bre*' says the Celt pointing to the hill. By way of explanation, the Saxon tells any subsequent Norman 'visitors' he comes from *Bre* on the *Dun*. To make things simpler for new residents, Normans coin the self-evident 'Bredon on the hill'. Hill, hill on the hill.

When asked where she'd come from, one performer at the last *plein air* publication launch who'd been delayed by trains replied 'Stardust'.

A performance of extracts from two visual poems what I wrote, with names for places translated from Welsh that fall somewhere between Stardust and hills on hills.

It features mild peril, on account of the Welsh titles.

Lleoedd dros dro

To the cold place from the hill, as the crow flies.

Hillside of the black crow
Hillside of the eagle
Enclosure of sunshine
Graves of the giants
Dwelling of the muse
A clearly-seen hill
Hill of contention
Hill of milk
Bubbles of the elan
Pass of the nun
Fort of refuge
Cairn of the goats
Place of hemlock
Crag of the warriors
Shelter from the sun
Stream with the sound of a bell
River, heard from afar
Court of the fox
Watching place
Robbers' meadow
Meadow of the tents
Haunt of the pony
Bare hill-top of the witch
Wood of the hermit

Recess of the salt water
Place of bees
Sacred place in the alders
Summer home of the cowhouse
Old winter home
Enchanted glade
Glade of the giants
Warm meadow
Meadow of the breeze
Grove of earliest times
Half-way dwelling
Edge of the wave
Bare hill of honey headland
Nest of the crow
Hollow of the teacher
Bird's end
Village of magpies
Village of the poets
Bridge of the blessed ones
Moorland of the servants
Ford of the confluences
Ledge of the raven
The cold place.

Cartref caret

The little roof at fair venture's end.

Home of the venture
House yonder
Farthest house
Place of leeks
House of hollow
Quiet place
Nesting place
Beloved mansion of the river meadow
Mansion of winding stream
Home of the bare hill
Bare hill of the chief's fort
Windy homestead
Stone house of the chieftan
Hill farm of the stones
Homestead of the pigs
Cabin of the black slope
Moor of the home of graves
Willow home of pebbles
Fair nook
Homestead in the middle-land
Home of the villeins
Mottled house
House of skins
Bead-house on low ground

Cabin of the meadow of canes
Homestead of barley
Three houses of the oak
House under the oak tree
Home of the oak of the sons
Cottage of the hole
Homestead of the streams
House of mud, home near the pool
Home in the big wood
Home of wild pigeon
Cottage of the short wood
Yonder village
Home of song
Wilderness retreat
Resting place
Little roof
Warm house
Pleasant place
Fair end.

NON PLUS ULTRA

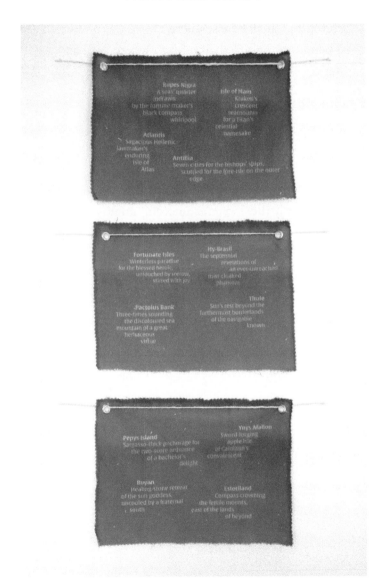

For context, I am presently here – on an island.
Presently, I shall be elsewhere.
When I am there, I shall refer to where I am as
'here'.

Imminently, we shall be on the plane of
immanence
Where all is all and there is everything beyond
Where thisness is all that is
And from which each and everything is composed
Consistently there even if unseen, unknown.

Plus ultra

Like nomads of the Thousand Plateaus who
know only latitudes and longitudes, we shall tell of
connections, becoming, speeds and haecceities.

Marks are a sign of wellbeing, and we shall find
there marks from the well of all being.

> Sword-forging apple isle of Camlann's
> convalescent – *Ynys Afallon.*

Alpha et omega
The first and the last
The beginning and the end

It's a mystery

    something difficult or impossible to
    understand or explain

    the secret rites to which only initiates are
    admitted

    the Eucharist

    a handicraft or trade

Alpha

In this beginning was the word

And the word became land

    'This is an [island], that is, the figure of an
    [island]. A figure, however, there could not have
    been, unless there were first a veritable [island].
    An empty thing, or phantom, is incapable of a
    figure'

    'the thing that is signified is effected by its sign'

    'in, with, and under the forms.'

    Sargasso-thick anchorage for the two-score
ordnance of a bachelor's delight – *Pepys Island.*

An island emerges when it cleaves from land or
lava, calves from ice...

and becomes known, when a sailor says what
they see...
or a painter, printer or poet puts marks on
material.

Do you say what you see, or see what you say?
Depends on your point of view.
Say, what do you see?

Isle is an isle is an isle is an isle

> 'The poet could use the name of the thing and
> the thing was really there'

> ' ... There cannot be several things exactly the
> same, for in that case there would not be several
> things, but the same thing itself. Therefore all
> things both agree with and differ from one
> another'.

> Kraken's crescent seamounts, for a Titan's
> celestial namesake – *Isle of Mam.*

It's all a bit of a mystery

Printing is a mystery – from beginning to end.

A seas' quartet, indrawn by the fortune-maker's
black compass whirlpool – *Rupes Nigra.*

In the manufacture of printers' metal type, a
matrix is the mould used to cast a letter – from the
Latin meaning womb or a female breeding animal.

Plus ultra

Our matrix-born font is the fount for all the
knowledge – where alpha and omega prevail as
glyphs – the fount of all answers from first to last
From the French for casting, and Latin for melt

Healing-stone retreat of the sun goddess, uncooled
by a fraternal south – *Buyan.*

Each glyph must be even in appearance with every
other glyph regardless of order or sequence.

Each glyph consists not only of the shape of the
character, but also the white space around it.

The white space of an iceberg was oftentimes
mistaken for an island.

Icebergs are formed when ice lands are calved…
like the heifer-born

Calved like the type that tells of its birth from the
matrix-womb

Tabular ice islands break from a shelf, to join the
blocky, dome, wedge, dry-dock and pinnacle.

Seven cities for the bishops' ships, scuttled for the
fore-isle on the outer edge – *Antillia.*

Icebergs are generally white because they are
covered in snow, but can be green, blue, yellow,
black, striped, even rainbow-coloured. Seawater,
algae and 'Bergie Seltzer' can create diverse
colours.

Three-time sounding the discoloured sea mountain
of a great herbaceous virtue – *Pactolus Bank.*

It is sediment and sea-floor drag that alloy the
bright to a dirty black
As type is alloyed to a lustrous grey metalloid, by
lead, tin and antimony

From type to tale is the thaumaturge's
wonderworking

An alchemist's journey from basest materials to
Archimede's votive gold coronation

Proof
Beyond doubt
Beyond belief

Sun's rest beyond the furthermost borderlands of
the navigable known – *Thule.*

Eureka! I have found it!
One hundred per cent proof
Ninety per cent invisible

If the bitty-berg calf is all but invisible but for its tithe
is a verse-berg tale but a tenth of its truth to tell?

Compass crowning the fertile mounts, east of the
lands of beyond – *Estotiland.*

Any immersed object is buoyed up by a force equal
to the weight of what is displaced by the object
Estimable density, inestimable depth.

Plus ultra

Has this all been but a mystery, from beginning to
end?

The septennial revelations of an ever-unreached
mist-cloaked phantom – *Hy-Brasil.*

Is there really nothing beyond the navigable
known?

Cleave – to separate, and to join

As if a 'berg from water, it is generally easier to *lift*
meaning, than to *pull it out*

Omega

Soon as read
Soon as melted

> Winterless paradise for the blessed heroic,
> untouched by sorrow, stirred with joy –
> *Fortunate Isles.*

Cleaving – to re-join waters from which icebergs,
the hot type's quench and our islands emerge

Glyphs, redistributed

The printer's devil takes the worn and broken type
to the hellbox for melting and recasting

Stories of all isles join the isles from all stories...
and all stories

All always part of all

Our all in all

All in all

Plus ultra

The Sagacious Hellenic lawmaker's enduring isle of
Atlas – *Atlantis.*

Do this in remembrance.

ABBREVIATIONS

To be brief, Steven's brief was to be brief.
So, however disappointing for you all, I'm aiming
to be on brief, by being brief.
And Steven shall become Steve.

If brevity is the soul of wit, it's touching that it's
coined in the *Ship of Fools*, 1509... a little after
three o'clock.

Briefly, too, I like Sol LeWitt – an innovator of the
'artist's book' and for our purposes here, just like
me, a minimalist.

But, as Don Quixote has it, 'the rest I should omit,
because length begets loathing'.

Chiefly, briefly, the adjective, or adj., 'brief'
was coined before 1200 as *bref* in *Arthour and
Merlin*, borrowed from Old French and directly
from Latin – brevis – for short... and it's spent
time in Romantic, Germanic and Icelandic
mouths through time, to refer to the shortest of
musical and written notes, a summary, or to give
information – a brief.

And it takes its place as a 'doublet' of 'abridge',
meaning curtail or lessen, borrowed from the Old

French – make brief.

Now, briefly, a 'doublet', ironically, can mean something doubled – altogether not brief then – in a linguistic sense: two or more different words from the same source.

The other in that doublet is 'abbreviation': a noun, n., coined probably by 1425 (just before half past two) – via Middle French from Latin – to shorten, make brief.

So, to put it briefly, at length we've arrived at abbreviation.

Abbreviation is abbreviated: abbr. not abb. which is abbey or the Italian *abbuono* for allowance or, interestingly in this context, discount.

For brevity's sake then, I'll abbreviate, because IMHO I've got a GSOH.

For context we're presently *ad init.* At the beginning.
Presently we'll be *ad fini.*, near the end, which will no doubt feel like *ad inf.*, at infinity.

It's nice to be *ad hunc locum,* at this place, but might be fun to follow where my BR, book of reference, leads... keeping it short has been harder than I thought.

Not sure whether I'm keen to learn whether the blood sugar, breath sounds and breaking strain of below-specification Bristol Boy Scouts in the Budgerigar Society, is more blessed sacrament than bullshit...

Or whether it's preferable to secure some balanced salt solution that meets the basic safety standards of the British Sailors' Society, to treat the boatswain sub-lieutenant's bacterial skin lesion... or a British Standard-size tub of lotion... sorry, lot.

Instead, I think I should default to British Sign Language and ask the Bachelor of Sacred Literature, in Latin old style perhaps, about the Law of the Seas, where line of sight is presumably required to prevent any loss of signal...

... so our Spanish gentleman captain can pause his cruiser for a canto, to charm a carboniferous cardinal's cold Celtic castle, with only Christ for confessor and cocaine for company. That one's copyright for a century.

Might we, with double hard hands and a high-grade holy ghost, retire to the dining room for the dead reckoning of some dynamic relaxation, after some digital rectal examination from the Director of Religious Education.

Finding our way to BURMA, we hope, before
the burp... be undressed ready my angel, for fear
I will leave you a bankrupt unemployed rejected
person...

Never mind, the great and good await, or perhaps
a grand, gilt-gold guide, or grey-green guardian
goalkeeper – ever-facing the goal attack of the
government actuary on general assignment,
dispensing general anaesthetic to the graphic arts.

Might instead we find a fellow fast family fighter,
with a cold, false, foolscap folio, for the fine art
of filtered air, fatty acid and Fanny Adams – a
fluorescent antibody of fuck all in Stoke-on-Trent.

Or what the L... a large Latin law learner
drawing the light, linear, line that links London,
Loughborough and Luxembourg to stage left...
where might we now in gentle paralysis make
general pause for the grand passion... for our
galley proofs have arrived for the sign SJF is
holding: TL;DR...

So, to discharge my entertainments duty with
an effective dose, measured by the experimental
detector, an extensive disease renders our existence
doubtful, and we've arrived at the acceptable daily

intake and one ABF – an absolute bloody final (drink), because it's OK, we're *ad fin.*, at the end.

Besides, we're POETS, we can all piss off early for tomorrow's Saturday, and it's TTFN and BBS...

Ta-ta for now, but let's be back soon.

nature nurture

NATURE, NURTURE

[Wearing a black bowler hat representing nurture, carrying a green bowler hat to represent nature]

Something elaborating on a visual poem what I wrote for *Seen as Read*: Nature, nurture.

For context, I am presently Nurture.

Presently, I shall be Nature.

[Exchanging the black for the green hat]

As Nature I shall, naturally, say some words
It's in my nature
It's only natural

In the beginning, the word. Tabula rasa. Well... two words.

An absence of preconceived ideas or predetermined goals, a clean slate.

Literally 'a scraped tablet'... with the writing erased...

So, before us and the word, then, was writing.
So, the word.
In the beginning was the word. Word was made
flesh. That flesh, amongst other things, had the
authority to name all the things the heavenly hosts
didn't know the names of. Like...

'Nature' – first up in the books of words:

> the phenomena of the physical world,
> including plants, animals, the landscape and
> other features and products of the earth, as
> opposed to humans or human creations...
> then...
> the basic features, character, or qualities of a
> person or animal
> inborn or hereditary characteristics as an
> influence on personality...

Can't resist it... it's all about us... how can we
redeem ourselves?

Nature's been with us
For ever
But the word? Not coined in English until 1275,
for the 'restorative powers of the body': it's from
the Latin for birth and character.

Later, we're getting somewhere, it's become
'innate character and creative power or impulse'
... although it's taken us until the late fourteenth
century.

Nature's often contrasted with Nurture,

 [Exchanging the green for the black hat]

something we stopped off to name at a similar
time... ages ago:

> to care for and protect someone or
> something while they are growing
> help or encourage development
> to cherish – an ambition, belief or hope
> upbringing, education, and the environment
> influencing personality... as opposed to
> inborn characteristics...

So... coined to make it all about us – only a
little after 'nature', which has little to do with us,
naturally – but even before then it was a surname:
Nurtur.

Really, is it all about names?
'we are all what nature and nurture have made us'
But which contributes more to the area of a
rectangle – its length or its width?
Sounds like it's all contested territory, of no

concern for us
For Nature knows a rose is a rose...

... and all the poet need do is use the name of the thing and the thing was really there... a rose is a rose, smelling sweet by whatever name.

Some names of roses... from a selected list of varieties, most suitable for any particular purpose... published by The National Rose Society in 1964 – the year of my own naming – nurture's take on nature... and surnames:

Alberic Barbier
Betty Uprichard
William Lobb
Ena Harkness
Ritter von Barmstede
Lucy Cramphorn
Meg Merrilees
Frau Dagma Hastrup
Stella
Uncle Walter
Violinista Costa
Faust

Here's a thing. A 'cultural or human universal' is a pattern, trait or institution common to all human cultures worldwide. Taken together this is the 'human condition'.

How far these are 'cultural' or inherited is 'nature versus nurture'.

It's contested, but I'm wearing a hat, we're poets and a rose is a rose.

Some of those things for which there's no known exception in the whole wide world:

> classifying age, colours, behaviour, body parts, fauna, flora, inner states, kin, sex, space, tools, weather conditions
>
> rites of passage, death rituals and mourning
>
> cooking
>
> personal names
>
> abstraction
>
> figurative speech, metaphors, symbolism
>
> special speech for special occasions and prestige from the proficient use of language like... poetry
>
> feeling and expressing affection
>
> triangular awareness... er... relationships with two other people
>
> copulation is normally conducted in privacy
>
> shame
>
> play and toys, beliefs and narratives, and

magical thinking to increase life and win love
art and poetry...

and... hairstyles, containers, visiting, and
attempts to control the weather

and males on average travel greater distances
over their lifetime.

[Exchanging the black for the green hat]

So, if the poet can use the name of a thing, and it's
really there... here are some names *for* roses:

Picture, The People, Brilliant, Optimist
Lively, Bashful, Buccaneer
Mischief... Grumpy, Firecracker
Oh La La
Dominator, Siren
Scandal
Pax
Circus
Miracle Enterprise
Parade, Serenade
Sleepy, Simple Simon
Dearest, Celestial, Angel Wings

and, with Joyfulness and Peace... 'the name of the
rose is meaningful to the understanding, although
there are now no roses remaining'.

Riddle	1.	2.	3.
A			
B			
C			
D			
E			
F			
G			
H			
I			
J			
K			
L			
M			
N			
O			
Ω			

QUESTIONNAIRE

(with Freke Räihä)

[While a questionnaire answer sheet is distributed]

In line with European Poetry Festival protocols about diversity, openness and honesty, everyone attending has to complete a questionnaire.

In the spirit of collaboration, Freke and I have completed one between us to help you with yours.

Tick the box to opt out of any imaginary prize draw.

No intellect was harmed during the preparation.

Names haven't been changed because no one is innocent.

Prove you are not a robot.

Terms and Conditions apply.

Question A.

How about the ocean?

1. Uncertain about the difference between ocean and sea, but my Bonnie lies over both, apparently.
2. Conflicted: I was press-ganged.
3. Probably churlish not to love it, but thinking of large bodies of water makes my tummy feel funny. I'll get back to you.

Question B.

Looking forward?

1. Forward is more than just momentum, yes, the front end facing the horizon.
2. Come to think of it …
3. Only when watching the cities burn.

Question C.

Say what you see, or see what you say?

1. You say: pay attention, but I am not paying for anything.
2. The window is facing: a) the sky, b) the street, c) the abyss.
3. Sometimes there is an answer embedded in the question, like a variance.

Question D.

Folk?

1. Spoon.
2. Rainbrowser.
3. Words are mere vessels made up using roots and concrete.

Question E.

Will there be anything left when corporate assured destruction has had its way?

1. Asymmetric small print suggests there's higher than average risk of adverse selection and moral hazard. Check your premium.
2. Will there be anything right?
3. Folk (Folk!).

Question F.

Do you have a name?

1. I do, thanks for asking. Aside from being troubled by the eternal concern about letting someone have your true name lest it affords them power over you, it's interesting how uneasy I remain without some compelling reassurance that there'll not be some other seemingly innocent questions further down, and the whole thing is designed simply to harvest my personal data. But, given there's been nothing yet to suggest that's the case, I'll tell you. It's Rumpelstiltskin.
2. The poet could use the name of the thing, and the thing was really there.
3. Simon is my given name. I didn't take it or anything. Saints' names were popular for 1960s new-borns. I know few other Simons and they're typically my age or the evil villain in adventure films. Although less frequently the evil villains, see also: Mark, John, Peter, Paul, David, Andrew and Matthew.

Question G.

How do you do?

1. New York City is a graveyard?
2. There are things. But they will not last.
3. Only in the sentimental memory of late Soviet Russia.

Question H.

This is not a question, yes?

1. Ooh! Ooh! don't tell me, let me guess... I love trick questions...
2. Fresh back from the Plane of Immanence, our hero has plenty on his plate.
3. Why, this be an answer, were it so?

Question I.

Who am I?

1. See answers 1 and 3 at Question F. I'm worried about you being harvested.
2. Is that a ruin in your pocket? Or are you just happy to see me?
3. I've had a good harvest – incessantly walking to avoid a shave, baking tales of alienation. But can you explain 'ergodic' please?

Question K.

I can see him.

1. He's neither small, nor far away.
2. Rest, I say, rest. Rest those tired eyes, those deceptive portals. Rest, I say, rest.
3. He's behind me, isn't he? Is he doing the 'bunny ears' thing?

Question L.

How do you think it's going?

1. I heard of a waltz. I think the waltz paraphrased Dylan Thomas.
2. It is a peach cobbler.
3. Sometimes I worry.

Question M.

Rebel against the gods' destiny, future world ruler, or fictional person in an already finished story?

1. It could be. The thesis that all is done (done for) might also be a sad trope.
2. Only sad girls are part of the revolution. Only sad boys, and the rest of us, are parts of revolution.
3. The revolution will not be televised; the revolution will be a crumpled paper.

Question N.

I've gone back over this and am unsettled by the underlying assumption of Question G – we're human beings, not doings. So, how do you be?

1. I am root. No, rot. Rot is the underlying assumption. Rot is doing just fine, rotting away. Rot is the relation; the roots must be airborne waving.
2. Doo-be-de-doo.
3. I am not so sure about the human thing. Things? Human feels.

Question O.

Were we right to assume he wanted us to 'work jointly on an activity or project' rather than 'cooperate traitorously with an enemy'?

1. I cannot remember for the life of me.
2. Enemy is the new black.
3. There is no such 'he'; he is an abstraction late in the Anthropocene.

Question Omega.

I beg of you to end this. Is that even a question? I miss Gertrude Stein. I miss Edouard Glissant.

1. Rose is a rose is a rose is a rose.
2. I fear we have gone cockamamie.
3. The name of the rose is meaningful to the understanding, although there are now no roses remaining.

NOTES

A little more about what, but mostly about where and when

What Am I Doing Here?

My summonings to attend and pay attention here, as elsewhere, are drawn from the fifteenth century banns of the Chester cycle of mystery plays, and from a Susan Sontag commencement ceremony speech from 2003 (Sontag, S., 2003. Turning Points. Irish Pages, 2(1), pp.186–191).

Bough, Bow, Bow

My first performed work, devised for the closing event of the third annual Writers' Centre visual literature exhibition at The Museum of Futures in Kingston on 5 March 2019. It is the only 'unscripted' piece in this collection and, like my contribution to the photopoetry-themed exhibition it celebrated, explores an abiding preoccupation with the hierarchy of trust we place in the marks and materials that writers and artists use to render meaning. The contextual reading given on bended knee is from Erik Roth's 'With a Bended Bow: Archery in Mediaeval and Renaissance Europe' (2012).

The Rose of the Name

Performed at the celebratory launch event of
'Poets Brut', a group exhibition of visual poetry
at the Poetry Society Café in London, on 8 July
2019. Apparently, roses were handed to the most
appropriate audience member for the name on
each flower's label.

It mines a diversity of material from the medieval
mind of Peter Abelard via Shakespeare to
The National Rose Society, and was my first
deployment of Gertrude Stein's tantalising play
with text and perception from 'Sacred Emily'
(1913). It was not my last.

Ego sum Alpha et Omega

I developed this novel ceremony, juxtaposing
paraphernalia and terminology from letterpress
printing and those from the spiritual canon, for the
ritual-themed Poem Brut at Rich Mix #5 on
13 July 2019.

As well as appearing here and there for me,
Titivillus can be found in several medieval dramas,
including the Wakefield cycle of mystery plays.
Here, it's a devotional fifteenth century treatise I'm
rendering in more contemporary English.

From further back, around the second century,

early Christian scholar Tertullian provides 'the figure of my body...' that you'll see me revisit, both in this form and as a conceit with other terms.

Memento Mori

Performed at a rather singular Writers' Centre Kingston literary happening on remembering our mortality and the benefits of death remembrance – 'Memento Mori: on Mortality' – at the Museum of Futures on 19 November 2019. I will never forget.

Reckoning Between the Lines

This performance and the visual poem it drew from were my contributions to 'Blockplay', a one-day pop-up exhibition and performance event at the Poetry Society Café on 8 December 2019. It was curated by what was then an emerging exhibition platform and occasional publisher of books and object poems, Poem Atlas. Now well-established and highly-regarded for its consistently generous work to stimulate and showcase innovative practice at the growing edge of contemporary visual literature, it has provided me with some transformative opportunities for my own practice that I shall ever treasure.

Blueprint for the Transcript of a Draft

Perhaps the closest yet to performed visual poetry:

a blueprint of the manuscript draft of a poem I had contributed to 'Poetry Illustrated, a Teenager's View' at the Royal Marsden Hospital, an exhibition of art by Sutton High School students responding to the work of poets in south west London.

I performed it for the opening of 2020's exhibition 'A Notational Literature, The (Un)finished Draft' at the Museum of Futures on 19 February 2020, one of the last public outings for many before the first national COVID-19 lockdown curtailed both exhibitions in which the poem found some form.

Some Material Considerations

The relaxing of some of the more restrictive pandemic measures in Spring 2021 provided the opportunity for a handful of members of PoPoGrou, a new collective emerging from SJ Fowler's online poetry programmes in lockdown, to perform at 'A History of Unnecessary Developments', his joint exhibition with Tereza Stehlikova at Willesden Library Gallery (on 23 April).

Chiming with the exhibition's theme, 'Some Material Considerations' uses historical and contemporary voices telling of the significance of the Victorian waterworks at Seething Wells in Surbiton, and of the work to defend what has become a vivid ecological and heritage asset for the community from inappropriate development by its rapacious owners.

For more than 150 years, securing a fitting future for the site has depended on people working with words. Alongside nineteenth century engineers and commentators, the site's current owners, planning inspectors and QCs, I speak here as I did in a public inquiry as advocate for The Friends of Seething Wells, when the site owner appealed against the local council's decision to refuse planning permission for its residential and leisure development on this extensively protected stretch of metropolitan open land. Roxy Music's 'Grey Lagoons' soundtracked our success.

There's much that's here and more you'll find from the Victorian commentators, waterworks engineer James Simpson and Dr. John Snow's grand experiment at www.seethingwellswater.org, as well as from Howard Benge, my research and campaign compatriot, in his 'Seething Wells, Surbiton' (2013), Surrey History, Vol XII.

There's more on the 'relaxed approach...' in the transcript of the High Court's hearing of NGM Sustainable Developments Ltd v. Wallis & Ors (22 July, 2015).

Documents associated with the refused planning application (11/16502/FUL) and subsequent appeal (APP/Z5630/A/13/2197943) are available from Kingston council (www.kingston.gov.uk/applications/comment-planning-application).

Origins

Composed originally for the celebratory launch of Poem Atlas/Corrupted Poetry's visual poetry exhibition 'Temporary Spaces' at the Poetry Society Café on 20 January 2020, this subsequently featured in text form online as part of a collaboration with Writers' Centre Kingston/ The Bradbury day centre, for Stanley Picker Fellow Ben Judd's 'The Origin'. The project reflected on Britain's island status and how islands shape the communities that live on them and resulted in an exhibition at Stanley Picker Gallery at Kingston University, at which this version was performed on 11 June 2020. The performance featured *'Lore ci-devant'* as a prop, the visual poem object I'd created for The Origin. Stanley Rogers' *Sea-Lore* (1929, Harrap) provided some sights and sounds from sailors at sea.

Laying Claim

Laying Claim draws on a visual poem I devised for SJ Fowler's online programme *Seen as Read,* and I first performed it on the Fairfield Recreation Ground in Kingston on 11 June 2021, to celebrate the launch of his *Sticker Poems* (Trickhouse Press, 2021).

As audience numbers had been greatly diminished by a significant disruption to public transport on the day, I reprised it in the revised form here for the contributors' launch of *Seen as Read* – the anthology of visual poetries emerging from the online programme – at Open Ealing in London, on 14 August 2021.

It is here that Nicholas of Cusa (1431–1464) first shares with me his singular insight on singular things that I frequently find fruitful.

Here and There

Drawing on a series of my visual poems using place names that reflect Welsh communities' intimate poetic relationships with the time, place and history they have shared, this was performed in Richmond Park in London on 1 July 2021. This *en plein air* Writers' Centre Kingston event for the European Poetry Festival launched several publications in Sampson Low's ongoing Poem Brut series.

Non Plus Ultra

This drew on research for the visual poem triptych I devised for Poem Atlas's first international exhibition, at the Art Park on Rhodes, Greece. 'Text-Isles' ran from 17–24 September 2021, and featured work from UK-based poets examining materiality through the lens of text and textiles. I'll be forever grateful to my dear friend and songsmith, Tobias Ben Jacob, for his introduction to the ontology of French philospher Gilles Deleuze, whose plane of immanence I first visit here with the metaphysical map he made with psychoanalyst Féliz Guattari (A Thousand Plateaus, 1980). I've been back since. The huge privilege of performing at the celebratory exhibition launch on 18 September provided a rare opportunity to bring together and explore at more than usual length some of those persistent preoccupations of my practice that you'll find throughout this collection.

Abbreviations

A Poem Brut performance on 15 October 2021, to launch SJ Fowler's Bastard Poems (Steel Incisors, 2021) and celebrate the generous community-focused endeavours of our host, Eachwhat Industries, in their new public studio premises in Bristol.

Nature, nurture

Part of Writers' Kingston Event #44, this celebrated the public launch of the Seen as Read anthology at The Town House, Kingston University, on 19 October 2021. It rehearsed elements of some age-long debates about the relative contributions nature and nurture might make to personal development, and pivoted around one of my seven visual poems in the anthology.

Questionnaire

My first collaboration, commissioned for the European Poetry Festival's celebration of Swedish poetry at The Town House, Kingston University, on 25 November 2021. 'Questionnaire' evolved over several weeks of online exchange with innovative Swedish poet and performer Freke Räihä, who I met for the first time moments before we took to the floor to perform. We became quickly confident it would not be the last time we work together and the hugely enjoyable experience represents a milestone in the evolution of my practice that feels a fitting way to close this collection of my work.

You can currently find videos of my performances at www.tyrrellknot.com.

I always laugh at some point in Simon's performances. When I watch them back on video, I am almost distracted by the sound of my own laughter. I laugh even though these performances are also intense meditations on the possible meanings of verbal patterning, and I laugh despite the seriousness of their underlying concern with linguistic relationships and language communities.

The performances are often very funny but that's still not why I laugh. I mainly laugh out of the sheer surprise and delight produced by the extraordinary balances, handsprings and revelations of Simon's linguistic dexterity.

Part archaeological adventure to retrieve lost verbal treasure and part magic trick, Simon's etymologies and histories become an incantatory love song to language. This is not a blind love, it is an open-eyed, knowing hymn to language's slippery seductions and sleights of hand. And, although I miss the mesmerising hand gestures and showmanship of Simon's live performances, this is of course why they work so well on the page.

Simon's documentation spreads out on the page the linguistic synapses of his live performances as textual relationships.

The magic still holds as Simon's word-play becomes more apparent and yet retains its plausibility, persuading us to look beyond semantic connections and meanings and to find, instead, a wisdom emerging from the material connections between his words. Something almost occult almost emerges in the spaces on the page as it does in the live performances, and this is why I laugh, seeing both the trick and yet also the glimpse of real magic that only a true magician can deliver.

Susie Campbell

'I am a poet, and this is my hat.'

To watch one of Simon's performances is to be dragged into a whirlpool of language – proceeding via semiotics and semantics, linguistics and etymology, he inhales meagre sound and exhales a cornucopia of resonance, a smorgasbord of reference.

His performance style has something of the music hall: the whimsy of hats and props, the beautiful pronunciation, the exaggerated gesture, the enthusiastic delivery. He speaks with wit and charm of numismatics, of comics and coins, of catalogues, of place names, of the sea and ships and wars, of the names of birds and flowers, and, most of all, of community.

Homonyms are stacked on homographs are piled on homophones to vertiginous effect, leaving the audience with a need to read the work, to untangle its complexity and revel in its revelations in their own time.

Martin Wakefield

ACKNOWLEDGEMENTS

It is the friendship and fellowship of those remarkable creative and productive folk that I speak of elsewhere that I'm keen to celebrate here.

To Lucy Furlong, Alban Low, Astra Papachristodoulou and Paul Hawkins, who have stoked some near-extinguished embers of writerly aspiration into the blaze that now warms my every day, and which Steven Fowler unerringly feeds and fans.

To other persistently permissive and playful PoPoGrou participants, Patrick Cosgrove, Ailsa Holland, Bob T. Bright, Chris Kerr, Lisa Blackwell, Laura Davis, Victoria Kaye, Sylee Gore, Stephen Sunderland and the multi-talented Susie Campbell and Martin Wakefield who so generously contributed their kind commentaries on the work you'll find staged on these pages.

To all these beautiful beings, whose encouragement, support and insight contributes so much to the evolution of my practice, I offer my deepest heartfelt thanks.

It's also been a particularly pertinent pleasure to have worked with such a talented team of Kingston University students to bring my performances to the page for Kingston University Press. To Aishwarya Rajak and Aríel Bertelsen, pursuing their masters in publishing, and Karin Markovič and Marisa Spence who are combining publishing with creative writing in their endeavour, I offer my thanks for the good-humoured creativity, commitment and professionalism I've so enjoyed throughout, and warmest wishes for a fruitful future in the field.

To my wife Helen and my daughter Lydia, with thanks for all things and all my love.

BIOGRAPHY

Simon Tyrrell is a writer and artist whose work celebrates the customary language, marks and symbols people have used to present, protect and promote their community and make sense of the relationships, time and space they share. He's a founder of The Museum of Futures in South West London and is a member of PoPoGrou.

He has performed and exhibited work at venues across London, in Bristol and Rhodes, and his work has been published by Sampson Low, Pamenar, Poem Atlas, Mellom Press, Kingston University, Penteract, UCL and Versopolis.

He wears a hat as occasion requires.

ABOUT KINGSTON UNIVERSITY PRESS

Kingston University Press has been publishing high-quality commercial and academic titles for over ten years. Our list has always reflected the diverse nature of the student and academic bodies at the university in ways that are designed to impact on debate, to hear new voices, to generate mutual understanding and to complement the values to which the university is committed.

Increasingly the books we publish are produced by students on the MA Publishing and BA Publishing courses, often working with partner organisations to bring projects to life. While keeping true to our original mission, and maintaining our wide-ranging backlist titles, our most recent publishing focuses on bringing to the fore voices that reflect and appeal to our community at the university as well as the wider reading community of readers and writers in the UK and beyond.

@KU_press

This book was edited, designed, typeset and produced by students on the MA Publishing course at Kingston University, London.

To find out more about our hands-on, professionally focused and flexible MA and BA programmes please visit:

www.kingston.ac.uk
www.kingstonpublishing.wordpress.com
@kingstonjourno

9 781909 362642